GRANT JONES

IN LOVE WITH YOUR PLACE

Caring for the Land and Each Other

Skookumchuck Press
Pioneer Square
Seattle

"These poems honor and celebrate the intimate relationship and history between human love and the landscapes where we make our lives."

Mike Robinson, Dash Point

Landscapes have always reached out to me. I feel the passion for life inside them, and this has given me the words to become very attached to the landscapes of my Mother Earth. Like all living things, landscapes need partners. They need caretakers to appreciate their expressiveness and stewards to reciprocate with them to increase their energy and fullness at every scale from the garden to the region. I put this book together to celebrate my love affair with the landscape and to capture the magnetism possible between its partners. The title pretty much says it all. This book is not a book of love poetry, although there are a few poems in it that I wrote to women I loved. The land gives me a voice, so this book also contains a few poems written by particular landscapes toward their surrounding landscapes, as well as poems between particular landscapes and particular people.

Grant Jones, Coyote Springs Farm

IN LOVE WITH YOUR PLACE

Caring for the Land and Each Other

Dedication:

I dedicate these poems to all those who are in love with their places and strive to protect them. I wrote this book to recognize my friends and neighbors who write poems to celebrate their attachments to the land and to the communities they love. I would never have become connected to many incredible landscapes of the Earth if it were not for my clients, colleagues, and friends. They inspired me. During my tenure as Director of Education of the LAF (Landscape Architecture Foundation), I took it upon myself to visit and lecture at thirty-five schools of landscape architecture in the Americas and to talk with students and faculty members. To them and all who follow after them, I offer this book as inspiration and support to all LAF Olmsted Scholarship recipients. It is their sinuous stewardship and passion to serve the Earth as its partner that I wish to honor.

Acknowledgements:

I wish to give special thanks to my old friend and fellow Roethke Advanced Verse Writing classmate, Mike Robinson, Tacoma poet, teacher, newspaper writer and fly fisherman, for his editorial craftsmanship of these poems; also my colleague at Jones & Jones, Emily Fong, for her assistance with book design; and to my wife, Chong-hui, for her unending support and infallible wisdom. Also, thanks to Chong for her pencil sketch of the swallow on page 20.

Publisher's Note:

To my friend Walter Henze, co-founder with me of the Okanogan Land Trust's Poetry Potlucks we've held the last nine years, and co-editor with me of *Okanogan Poems Volume 3*, I extend profound thanks. His design and management skills were essential in expediting the printing and distribution of this book through the CreateSpace Team at Amazon.

I made the first selection of these poems while living at the KIm-Oya house in Otobegaoka, Toyota, Aichi Prefecture, Japan during December 2013. I made the final selection at Coyote Springs Farm in February 2017.

Grant Jones, Publisher
Skookumchuck Press
Pioneer Square
Jones & Jones, Ltd., 105 S. Main Street, Suite 300, Seattle, WA 98104

Copyright © 2018 by Skookumchuck Press and Grant Jones
All rights reserved. No part of this book may be used or reproduced in any manner whatsoever without the written permission of the Publisher, except in the case of brief quotations embodied in critical articles and reviews.

ISBN: 978-0-9796495-6-1

IN LOVE WITH YOUR PLACE

Caring for the Land and Each Other

"What are the natural features which make a township handsome? A river, with its waterfalls and meadows, a lake, a hill, a cliff or individual rocks, a forest, and ancient trees standing singly. Such things are beautiful; they have a high use which dollars and cents never represent. If the inhabitants of a town were wise, they would seek to preserve these things, though at a considerable expense; for such things educate far more than any hired teachers or preachers, or any at the present recognized system of school education."

        Henry David Thoreau, *Journal*

**Coyote Springs Farm at the mouth of the Canyon of the Little Mosquito
Looking northwest toward Whisky Mountain and the confluence of the
Similkameen and Okanogan Rivers in the Oroville-Osoyoos Gap between
the North Cascades and the Okanogan Highlands at the border with Canada.**

"Every landscape has its code, and if you fall in love with it and give it a voice, the poems you unearth from it will forever give you a place to stand as partner and friend and lover."   GRJ

CONTENTS

THERE ARE WORDS

Memory Number One
2

Chasing Eskers up the Tyone
3

Running from Pizarro
4

The Whisky Mountain Fire
6

When My River Becomes a Beaver Pond
7

Transformations
8

Tributaries Wait
9

Amazon Drift
10

Love In the Right Time
11

Her Roots Run Deep
12

Returning to the Drop Off
13

Land of Fires
15

Skies over the Grande Ronde
16

There Are Words Hay Palabras
18

BIRDS SEEM TO KNOW YOU

Irish Fields Pulse
22

Trout Dreaming
23

Skagit Flowers for Sasquatch
24

Tiger and the Rabbit at Sunrise Meadows
25

If You Asked Me How Love Can Happen
26

Leaving for Melbourne
27

A Smile In the Laugharne Marshes
28

Spring Up the Methow
30

Pools of Honey
31

When the Hay Smells Just Right
32

Tracking Moon Breath
33

A Two-Pocket Birthday
34

Beach Voice
35

Homo Tremuloides
36

Birds Seem to Know You
38

THE FOOTBRIDGE

Bathing in Chokecherries
42

A Song for Sarsapkin
43

Sometimes My Mind Goes Outside Itself
44

Memories that Stay On
45

Clovelly's Cyclone
46

A Night with the Saguaros
47

Kisses from the Highlands
49

The Footbridge
50

RIVERS HAVE A HEART

Braided River
54

Sleeping on Rocks
55

The Landscape of Love's Fruiting Mind
56

Open Thine Eyes: Talking to Beaverhead
57

Mapping Marriage Places
60

Strong As A Willow
61

You Bent My River
62

Falling in Love with the Land Is Not Too Easy to Explain
63

I've Been This Way All My life
65

Rivers Have a Heart
66

Spirit Visitors
67

At the River
68

Floodplain of the Tyone, tributary of the "Big Sue" in Central Alaska

THERE ARE WORDS

Your first dog can teach you how to find your life story in tall, blowing grass under the billowing cumulus clouds of summer. And so can a good bush pilot; he'll thread you in his Super Cub, a shuttlecock through the looms of Alaskan riverine landscapes. Afterwards, you'll have words you can use to walk the backs of mountains in the sky with ancient shepherds who dance and shamans who are always waiting for you to write your own story. The mountains themselves give you words too, but more than that they'll share their mountain feelings and the love they hold for each other. After a while, you'll think like a beaver able to transform rivers back into clouds. You'll also be able to swim across rivers at an angle with your lunch between your teeth and flush herons squawking from bank to bank. Other animals will teach you, such as how to hover like a condor before you cross a dune-hammock to the beach. Trees, of course, know even more and will share what they've seen with you. Alders and willows will give you knees and hands to hold cliffs back from falling. Old people don't have to talk to give you their meaning or to share their wisdom as the trees do. You'll find the radiant strength of a conductor as she lifts her symphony; and you'll find peace like a naturalist at rest under a tree on his overlook.

Memory Number One

When I was three, I rolled off my bedrail
And fell into infinity,
Gravity became my friend
And every night for years
I left this world for the sun;

But every morning my long haired Collie
Was my rudder and my shadow.
"Duke" licked back the hair from my eyes,
Pulled on my shirt like a jib
And tacked me through the shoulder-
High grass below the house, where
Granddad swung his scythe
Through tall breaths from his chest,
To lie down under the ancient Silver Poplar
And look up its trunk five stories
Where thousands of flashing leaves
Roared and soughed and whispered
To a steady salt-wind off the beach
And dreamed me into the clouds that coursed
Across Duke's orangey-brown eyes like liquid
Messages from the glaciers hanging off The Brothers,
My wolf-eared mountain was watching across the Sound.

Coyote Springs Farm
Mouth of the Canyon of the Little Mosquito
Okanogan Sub-Watershed
9 August 2014

Chasing Eskers up the Tyone

It doesn't look like the wolves will go hungry
on this low-sun night when the caribou are running
along the top of an esker, spooked by cloud shadows
that race across this landscape that has a mind of its own,
pulling its ancient horizons inside out,
forgetting to wake because it can't ever sleep.
Only a river that dreams can save itself up here.

As I this evening come along at the end of an all-day flight,
watching the creeks pass by under my Super Cub,
the Big Watana, the Oshetna, the Kosina,
the Jay, the Tsusena and now the Tyone
shadowed by this endless esker with the caribou
running along its top, about to be nabbed
by the waiting wolves who den up inside it,

I realize that this wandering river, the Tyone,
has been coming out of nowhere for a very long time
and has survived for eons always licking
a life for itself, as it dreams its destiny
just like the wolves in their dens waiting.

Tyone River
Upper Susitna River Basin
Alaska

Running from Pizarro

Sky Dance

There is a room on top of the world
Where the sky is long and low in the evening light,
Above a landscape of shifting cloud masses.

Burial towers, the chulpas of Sillustani, plunge skyward as
A young girl, spinning among sod clumps and ichu grasses,
Twirls out a *huayno* beneath a dark sky in heavy wind.

Under a driving hail, the old woman,
Her pollera, black, and orange wrap, and flap,
Herds her llamas back, back to her chacra,

Picking up stones throws them aside with one hand,
The other collects dung, rolled in her apron for a cold
Night's smoldering fire, as lightning shatters the sky

Above this ancient, stony landscape to strike the apachetas
Piled in devotion at each spot marking good luck,
To keep from getting tired, the traveler from cold,
As a funeral huddles in the boulders along the road.

Urubamba

From high stranded canyons, mist-swelled brims
That leak out at ends and bends,
The road unravels the slope and
Curls across the dark valley floor,
As trucks leave dust trails like turbots
Scuffing across a clear sandy bottom at noon;

When shadows lengthen, and this mountain glows
With its rhombic mustard-yellow fields,
In shapes of torn, wet blotters,
Algae green, like quilted clothes,
Joints overlapping like suture scars
In a potsherd collage of crumbling rock walls,

I climb up each hogback with my eyes,
Up the chains of strike-ridges that stretch from the valley floor
Like wandering funicular staircases
To the tall and scarified ice faces
Shining in the intense golden sun,
Gleaming pure as quartz or salt,
As my chest swells tight to be an Inca.

Puno and Urubamba
On the Urubamba River
El Peru
June 1967

The Whisky Mountain Fire
An Anniversary *Sijo* for Chong-hui

This afternoon Mount Hull,

Made love to Whisky Mountain,

And a fire from Carter Lakes

Burst out the mouth of her canyon

Licking four ridges before quelling

His loving rains foretelling.

Written at Coyote Springs Farm in the North Okanogan Valley
19 August 2007

When My River Becomes a Beaver Pond

I can't explain

your voice

your eyes

your hands

in these channeling moments

after you leave

when my river

becomes

a beaver pond.

Written in the beaver ponds eastside of the Methow below the pedestrian suspension bridge downstream of Mazama, North Cascades, Washington.

Transformations

The eagle in the tall broken fir on the island
Has been motionless except for his rotating head.
Earlier this morning he sailed in with the sun
On an updraft that lifted him over the cumulus pass
High above the mainland. It had never been felt
 in these parts before.

I felt like an island while you walked my shores
Climbed my cliffs, and glided across my meadows
Leaving marks in the grass, each place where you lay
In sun behind mossy hummocks, sheltered from wind;
Everywhere you touched my skin, my island
 wears your imprint.

There are rivers that flow from the same mountain,
That have never seen each other, but then suddenly join
Doubling themselves and filling up each other,
To commingle as if they knew, have known each other
 for a thousand years.

Written on Crane Island, San Juan County, Washington, August 29, 1999.

Tributaries Wait

Now...
when we're apart, each stronger than the last,
my emptiness expands like a gourd
grows in the evening after sun's warm parting,
leaving a deeper hole to fill each morning
as the shadows inch across my bare feet in the sand;

While...
these minutes pump through my heart like the river
remembers how we stood, straight,
hands fluttering like the cottonwoods swaying
at its confluence, leaves trembling in the wind;

As...
it waits for us to refill this tributary pool
with the imprint of our hearts each Spring
here where the Taylor and the Snoqualmie meet,
under the grandfather face of Garfield Mountain.

Written at the confluence of the Taylor River on the Middle Fork of the Snoqualmie, where the high rock crags along the granite face of Garfield Mountain shoot straight up from the narrow valley floor, making it look like a three-thousand-foot cathedral hewn out of the western flank of the North Cascades, 9 April 2003.

Amazon Drift

You flow, and seeming no control,
Flood, a huge, colossal flower;
Striving against your mud, seeking uniformity.

Your sky, cumulus, and heaving, bears a light
Most intense through piles of rising
Jungle clouds like immense lanterns.

Two hawks, *Buteo*, dark
Brown with creamy yellow wing patches, flocking
Parakeets chased by a pair of "capitáns," kingfishers,

While a large bird flies gracelessly across the bow
Like a giant chicken with buzzards' wings
And long falcon tail, a "camungo," a screamer.

Only one white porpoise all day, at three-thirty,
An evolutionary ghost, far from the Atlantic,
Signal for my genes to head home.

Aboard the Booth Line *MS Valienti*
Near Benjamin Constant on the Amazon
13 August 1967

Love at the Right Time

If I on the beach while, I'm sitting,
   lift my foot
   and the footprint holding
   this morning's yellow shade
      harbors a dozen sand fleas
      who hop out into bright rays of the sun
      and attract dragonfly
      whose mate follows
      across shallows along the shore,
      her shadow coursing over the water
      stirring minnows which lure sand dabs
      that great blue heron then spears for breakfast,

and if that footprint contains
   a shell which reminds me
   of the spiral curve of your eyelid
      causing me to gulp rasping air
      followed by a long audible sigh
      which wakes song sparrow in the brush at my back
      and makes her careen into the fir overhanging the eelgrass bed
      dislodging a fresh green cone which slowly sinks to the bottom
      attracting rock crab which otter on the bank then dives for,

and if my laughing breath containing all these feelings
   rises to mingle with the summer clouds
   whose billowy bellies you can almost touch,

then what is life
   but love at the right time
      all the way to the spinnaker of the moon.

Written on Jones Beach, Pole Pass, Crane Island, San Juan County, Wasp Islands, Central San Juan Islands Sub Region, San Juan Islands Region, The Salish Sea

Her Roots Are Deep
For Iona Belle Mendenhall Thomas Jones
January 15, 1903, Salem, Oregon--August 17, 1999, Seattle, Washington
1942-48

Above the beach
Among the fir trees
Lives now quietly,
Someone I know.

She stands contentedly
Waiting seasons' rearranging
Never aging
Never changing.

Her roots are deep
And hold her firmly,
As she comforts us all,
Branches swaying
Above now.

Her bloomings grace her
Her movements speak her,
Hold her perfect
Make her brighter
Than all I know.

We call her Mother
We call her kin;
We know she'll be with us
In the end.

Richmond Beach Tide Flats and Victor Jones Marsh Ponds, North Central Puget Sound, The Salish Sea, 1964.

Returning to the Drop Off

Alone, out early, before
the first bird cries,
before the gulls and fish crows
start plundering, I wade
alone to the outermost bar
a half mile offshore.

The bar's drying even before the sun breaks
And I can see the sand crystals split open
just above the clamshells,
like tiny mouths above each shell.

Each of these tiny refts marks a cockle,
a telltale crack,
to practiced eyes,
even etches a whole string of cockles, a reave
of morsels along the ridge of the sandbar.

Glaucous-winged gulls learn to see
these marks in the sand
during their lifetimes.
They cock their heads like robins
to hear whispers from a cockle
as it cracks open its shell.

A half inch from the surface,
a cockle becomes visible to me now.
A few deeper, faint double-eye cracks
appear that the gulls will miss
even though I see them plain.

But to be sure I scuffle off their tiny reaves
with my boot, so wise old gulls
will have to look for breakfast farther up the beach.

This outermost bar a half mile from shore
is really two bars;
a lagoon in between
leads to blue water.

Here, in the shallows,
fluid in the currents ebbing out
these two pristine glistening fingers,
in the dark green eelgrass that swirls
tangled with eel blennies that tickle
your calves as you make paths,
where sea perch dart curving kelp strands,
startling sand dabs who explode now between my toes,
the water is colder, and the bottom clear.

Wading deeper, licks shivers up my ribs
I begin to hear my young boy spirit
breathing deeply, suspended, lifting to a wave
at the calving edge of the drop off.

But wait, turn around. I'm too old for this
and my spirit needs to stay in its home in my chest.

Richmond Beach Tideflats at Point Wells two miles north of Boeing Creek
North Central Puget Sound Sub-Region
The Central Puget Sound Region
The Salish Sea
November 18, 2014

The Land of Fires

Sun breaks,   and wave fires flash.
The sky is blue,   blue as ice.
Flamingos paint   lagoons pink.
Gauchos flailing   black coats flap.
Glaciers in the clouds   like sails full-and-by,
Broad-reach the straits,   search how and why
A condor overtakes   its shadow on the ground.
With a shell to my ear   I hear the mouth of your soul.

El sol rompe,   y el fuego emana.
El cielo azul,   azul el hielo.
Los flamencos pintan   lagunas rosadas.
Los gauchos lanzan   sus abrigos negros al viento,
Los glaciares en las nubes   como velas al viento
Alcanzan los estrechos,   buscando la razón
El condor vuela   sombra en la tierra.
Y con una concha en mi oido   escucho la boca de tu ser.

Written May 22, 1994 at the mouth of the Río Condor, north of Puerto Arturo, on the Isla Grande, Chile, also known as Tierra del Fuego, the Land of Fires. I conceived the poem first in Spanish, then in English. I then collaborated with my old friend and colleague M. Mario Campos Campos to polish the Spanish version, and this reshaped the English. For this reason they need to be experienced as one.

Skies Over the Grande Ronde

Evening slowly settling...

Sunset above the balsamroots,
Penstemons and lupines,
Scorchy pink paint drops
Bursting on the surface
Of a languid lavender river.

And then at dawn...

Sunrise ripples
Across last night's starry sky;
As a half-moon swims
Down the delta's fanning
Branches of orange light
Like a skate in the estuary.

By midmorning...

Cottony clouds
Swim in drifts
Beneath tall white banks
Of alto cirrus
Plumes trail easterly
Like Appaloosa ponytails.

Everything speaks of horses...

Saddle Butte,
Corral Ridge,
Horsethief Canyon,
On these flat-topped buttes,
Ridges and flats
Flex and pump
Like withers and loins,
Pulsing between gulches,
As box canyons and hollows
Trot off to the horizon
In parallel waves
To the Wallowas
To the Seven Devil's Mountains in the south
And the Clearwater Mountains in the east.

After nightfall, the second day...

The air fills me
With cords of fire.
Something is so close
I can't see its shape,
But I feel it
Breathing behind my ears,
Like the wind carries whispers
From your heart.

Written at the Wenatchee Guard Station perched at 6050 feet on Menatchee Mountain, looking south and east over the Grand Ronde River, south of Pomeroy in Asotin County, Washington May 1997.

Hay Palabras - There Are Words

Hay palabras
   There are words
que cuentan la historia
   which tell the story
como hojas en la tierra
   like leaves on the ground
son mensajes.
   make messages.
Hay palabras
   There are words
doblandose como arboles en el viento
   like trees bending in the wind
que cuentan la historia
   which tell the story
de corazones no vencidos.
   of hearts holding on.
Hay palabras
   There are words
que cuentan la historia
   which tell the story
como las piedras que hacen las playas
   like small rocks making beaches
que cuentan historias silencios.
   speak histories.
Hay palabras
   There are words
que echan raices
   which root
y sostienen las montanas.
   and hold the hills from overturning.
Hay palabras.
   There are words.

Written at Partridge Point on Whidbey Island, Admiralty Inlet Sub-Region, North Sound Region, The Salish Sea Estuary
October 1995.

BIRDS SEEM TO KNOW YOU

Birds know more than you do, and they can feel the ground breathing into the turning of the stars. They are like trout watching you from their deep pools. You'll learn the words to recognize them as well as a lot of other beautiful things. Gorgeous things like raptors and shorebirds, bars and beaches, grandfather drift logs that floated down from the mountains to rest in the estuary, along with the ancient people who were born there, including the old Sasquatch who watched them. Whether you sleep on high mountains or fly in a plane to distant watersheds the other side of the world, the birds of each place you know will welcome and show you the way through their landscapes. The birds will introduce you to their complex social structures while sharing their ways, and this will help you learn your own local culture. These birds everywhere are practical, indomitable and don't complain. Their steadiness will calm you. Sometimes they can be ethereal though and you might want to sail to the moon. Above all, the birds are watching you, and they know you year after year after year.

Irish Fields Pulse

Under each field
A working heart swells
And slowly pulses
To the pendulum sun,

Like each new generation
Hangs up its moon
To breathe to sleep
On shimmering nights

Under lines of stars
That shift and draw out
Their special stories
From the slanting void.

Written on the Cork train between Portlaoise and Ballybrophy
November 7, 2006

Trout Dreaming

Each morning you walk across the cobblestones through the trees,
Like ankle deep water pouring
Over the rounded stones of a quiet mountain river.
You move as if trout know every pore of your body.

I will come to this place to imagine
Your figure gliding over the cobbles.
I'm a trout in a shady pool resting,
Dreaming your return.

Written in Occidental Square, Pioneer Square Historic District, Seattle, October 1996.

Skagit Flowers for Sasquatch

Walking straight in, toward the sun,
I scrambled across the ancient drift logs,
Some as old as the last Indian
Who knew the Sasquatch who lived
Across the delta on the bluffs above Utsalady,
Walking out into the full embrace
Of this enchanted landscape halfway
Between frogs and flounders and dragonflies
Of the ditches and the Caspian terns of the mud bars,
Halfway between this year's cedar logjams from the mountains
And the long banks of driftwood across the shores of big Skagit Bay,

I sat down on a log hummock at the head of a small guzzle
Leading into a salt creek that tracks off into the sunset,
To fill my eyes, now that there are these things
Like rippling sun streaks leaping across the delta,
Like rolling swirls of sandpipers in the tide sets,
Like streaming chains of geese across the bars...
Now that there are these times when birds say your name,
Now that there are these times when the thought of you
Bursts from the swaying grass like a harrier lifting the wind,
Now when words spring from my tongue
Like the flowers, you seeded in my heart.

Written out on the Skagit Bay Flats of Fir Island, which is the delta of the north and south distributaries of the Skagit River, just north of Utsalady on Camano Island, "Land of the Berries." This locale is the home of the Kikiallus Tribe of Coast Salish People. It was also recorded by the Duwamish to be the birthplace of the Sasquatch, 9 April 2005.

Tiger and Rabbit at Sunrise Meadows

Where mountains hang in the sky
Embraced by clouds of their mother's caress,
In a meadow of flowers
You were sleeping.

Afterward,
On my lips, you put glacier lilies
To quiet the fire of the sun
That lives inside me.

Written in the meadows just below Sunrise on Mt. Rainier, "Mountain of all Mountains", Tacobet to the Nisqually and Tacobud to the Puyallup, Tahoma to the Klickitat and Yakama. Twauk to the Skykomish, Ti'Swaq to the Duwamish, August 29, 1999.

If You Asked Me How Love Can Happen

And so if you asked me how love can happen
what love can emanate from,
I would tell you that I have seen it come in clouds,
in rivers, and from birds and the leaves
on trees, and from...you.

I would tell you that I have seen it contained
in dreams, springing out of sleep
like beautiful tigers from peaceful glades.
And from you in such force as rock becomes river,
as my soul flutters, swimming
with the dippers who work the eddies and riffles
flipping pebbles for mayflies,
as these memories tilt time while the river roars.

Written in West Seattle, 1 June 2000
Coyote Springs, 21 January 2014

Leaving for Melbourne

This evening, as we embraced,
saw the sun, set in the West,
felt our hearts turn from pink to gold,
it got easier and easier to say goodbye.
And now, leaving, every moment
opens its self in my heart.

Written climbing out over Vashon Island on a flight bound for Los Angeles,
then Melbourne, Victoria, Australia, April 1999.

A Smile for the Laugharne Marshes

This landscape knows me.
Old ladies ask me directions
When I go into town;
They see their smiles crowding my eyes.

When I wade down the Corran
Trousers wrapped round my neck
Skinny legs pulsing
In the deep thalweg of the channel,
I'm the heron who stands at the bends.

Out the muddy Taf
The wind flattens my hair, figures me a curlew
Blown in from the beaches off Barrynarbor,
Cross the Bristol Channel in North Devon.

I jump 28igante and reens past the Grist Mill.
Light shifts and I'm an oystercatcher.
I screech like an arrow along the sea cliff
Out the Laugharne Marshes—
Over footings of the Freething Ferry,
Past the mouth of Railsgate Kill,
To the baulked up sharestrips of Lee's Common.

That's where quiet as lichen
On a cast iron corner post, we rotate our heads,
A pair of kestrels weaving through the coppices,
We hug the swellings over Sir John's Hill,
Zag through those hillslope oaks
On down the other side, and we hide
In the brackens, corner of the farmer's bullmeadow.

Gaze, mirrors fused
Deep in the back of our eyes, ice shield melting,
Then we doze till dark, two travelers,
One, crowsfeet etched onto his temples,
Other, her boreal eyelids, half closed
Walking up the path to the house, behind the Castle.

The Corran Stream, watershed of the River Taf,
Laugharne Marshes, Sir John's Hill,
Laugharne Village, Carmarthenshire, Wales
August 31, 1999

Spring up the Methow

Aspens flash
Like your hair blows
And the wind fills my lungs
With all the midday implications
From these muscular hills
Bathed in their own sunlight of balsamroots
Lupines, penstemons,
And anise swallowtails.

Written on Gobbler's Ridge, above Wolf Creek in the Methow Valley, Winthrop, Washington May 1999.

Pools of Honey

Before I met my wife Chong-hui, I had never known anybody with golden eyes. From a distance, they could have been black. Up close they were deep pools of honey glinted with flecks of gold, like some agates are when they're wet, like a spoonful of molasses in green tea, even as in the sweet flesh of wild plums after you pull back their dark skin with your teeth. I could only wonder where this goldness came from, but now that it existed, I saw it everywhere in the landscape.

This morning in the towering palisades of the Columbia
Where Moses Coulee carves through the Waterville Plateau,
The basalt glowed like elongated, beeswax columns;
And on the outside face of this immense golden honeycomb,
White-throated swifts careened between the ramparts.
I had never known someone with golden eyes.

In reeds along the shores of Ancient Lake
In the northwestern potholes of Quincy Basin,
Yellow-headed blackbirds made singular, hoarse croaks
To claim their place in the midday sun,
While Ring-billed gulls floated quietly offshore.
Your eyes glistened like the wild plums at the old homestead.

High up the Icicle River under the Ponderosas above Snow Creek
Where the Balsamroots stain your boots golden yellow,
A Golden eagle dived onto the ample bosom
Of Sleeping Lady Mountain this evening,
As I sit by this river dancing with Dippers—
Your eyes are filling up with pools of honey.

Written on the second day of the North Cascades Institute's Spring Birders' Retreat, Sleeping Lady Mountain Retreat, Icicle River, Leavenworth, Washington, 12 June 1999.

When the Hay Smells Just Right

When the skin
  along the arch
    of your collarbone
      turns translucent
        like abalone shell,

When the bark
  of the alder
    is so silver
      it burns holes
        in your eyes,

When the cool black
  of the night
    wraps you
      with millions
        of crow feathers,

When the moon
  bathes your neck
    the way the dew
      kisses
        ripe apricots

  In the morning
    just before dawn
      when the hay
        smells just right,
          I'll remember you.

Written in West Seattle in September of 2003.

Tracking Moon Breath

Moonlight's braided
   swimming
      silk dress

Swirls around the trees,
   makes eddies like a creek
      lifting out of its banks;

And dances on air
   as each trailing breath
      carries love from our hearts.

Written at Mossycliff cabin on Crane Island, San Juan Islands Archipelago in The Salish Sea of Washington, 1 August 2004.

A Two-pocket Birthday

Chong-Hui is sewing two pockets with button flaps
in the lining of my favorite wool vest.
She scavenged them off a Liasport work shirt
she bought back in Seoul, made in Macedonia.

Little did she know back in Ninety-three
she'd marry a man from Seattle and spend green days
at his cabin among hummocks of yellow moss
under the craggy Grand firs of the Wasp Islands.

Or that one August she'd cut the pockets off
that old work shirt of hers and sew
them into his Pendleton Indian vest
for his birthday.

Written at Mossycliff cabin on Crane Island, San Juan Islands Archipelago in The Salish Sea of Washington, 29 August 2004.

Beach Voice

Wind rustles
        In the pines this morning.
                The way you murmur at first light.

When I walk on the beach
        Each cockleshell talks.
                It reminds me of your smile.

Every time I hear them
        I can't keep from laughing.
                Your voice rehearses with the waves.

Written at Jones Beach, Crane Island, Pole Pass, San Juan Islands Archipelago of The Salish Sea, Washington, August 2003.

Homo Tremuloides

1
How far did you blow (down from Kodiak?)
Before your seed found this sweet-water spring
Up the far head of East Sound?

2
How long had you soughed in the wind
Before you heard soft scraping of our skin boats in the sand
Beside the sleeping logs drifted down from the Yong Jang,
Now we call it the Amur.

3
How long did you wait on this back dune by the spring
Before you heard our cedar sail fluttering and fluttered back?
We flashed our paddles and smelled like cockles that walked.

4
For how long had you unhinged your leaves
Before we saw you blinking and blinked back at you?
We'd seen so many mirages on the ice that we were dumb.

5
You had made yourself delicious to many animal,
Ocean to mountain and prairie to muskeg.
But you needed men and women attracted to your beauty.
We began by leaving kisses scratched on your bark.

6
So for how long did you wait for the partner you made of us?
Your sensorous bark was dying in the firestorms,
But your roots you made to take it.
Out of respect, our old fires were small, not that hot.

7
Afterwards, you maxed your advanced quaking just for us,
All that flashing from five miles out
Followed by the whispering and trembling up close.

8
Maybe you were too much for us;
We wanted you to have everything.
Then all the newcomers came,
Distracted and dropped the ball.
Your beautiful quaking had made us your stewards,
But we'd forgotten to recognize our faces in the mirror.

Coyote Springs Farm
Little Mosquito Canyon of Aspens
Mosquito Creek-Okanogan Sub Watershed

In the San Juan Island Archipelago at the back of Swift Bay way up Orcas Island's East Sound, an ancient band of Quaking Aspen (Populus tremuloides) grows from the slightly elevated ridge of a sandy back dune, That back dune separates the driftwood shore of the bay from the freshwater swamp which is fed by a distributary of the creek delta behind. How those aspens formed this rare grove is a real mystery. The road to Mt. Constitution now cuts off the old beach-to-dune continuum, but quite likely there are middens still scattered along this aspen-strewn reach of the bay, relicts from a long-standing Indian village. However, without the fires of human stewards along the beach, the aspen are now being engulfed by firs and may die out. It appears that Quaking Aspen came to with the glaciers twenty thousand years ago and spread by the partnership with our human species (managed fire and seeding, both human and wind-borne) throughout the Americas beyond the Sierra Nevada as far as the Sierras of Baja California and the Sierra Oriental of Central Mexico. They are single-sexed (dioecious) with males generally found at high elevations and females in lower elevations, and are clonal (each grove a single individual of spreading ramets sprouting from the underground roots); their bark is vegetative and photosynthesizes just like leaves do making the bark non-resistant to fire, however dependant on human-set small, non-fatal fires that burn out the brush needing water. These small fires then lifted the water table and creeks reappeared, and the seeps expanded widening each aspen stand.. Aspen!... quaking for humans and fire and grass and elk and wolves and bears and bees and butterflies, ladybugs, and ants. And they're uniquely American.

Birds Seem to Know You

Sparrows build
      Woven nests each spring
            When your smile outplumbs the moon.

Seagulls slant
      Down slopes of wind
            When you walk through the forest to the beach.

Birds seem to know you,
      Before they see you.
            I think what they see is the light

That sings off your forehead,
      Shoots through branches;
            Blue-green halos are hanging in the trees.

Written at Mosscliff cabin and Jones Beach, Crane Island, Pole Pass, San Juan Island Archipelago of the Salish Sea, July 2001

THE FOOTBRIDGE

Simple things become most sacred. The overhanging tree becomes a haven for your deepest feelings. A valley where you live can arch your heart and soul and transport you wide awake in your dreams and in that way your valley will link you to distant places where you can be with friends. You can learn to talk with other living things like trees that are always waiting and to interpret their stories. You can talk with those who are gone and honor their spirits still residing under the trees in certain places. You become a bridge and never have to leave your place to go anywhere.

Bathing with Chokecherries

When you were bathing in the horse trough this morning
Cranking on the pitcher pump to rinse your long hair
As fat white blossoms, falling from the Chokecherries
Overhanging the old homestead well
Drew out your contours scenting the granite cold water,
I had to smile to myself for being alive.
There was just no way to bottle that scene.

Written at the old William E. Peterson well at Coyote Springs Farm, North Okanogan Valley, Washington, 19 June 2010.

A Song for Sarsapkin

Soaring birds break
Your skin of day
Stretched translucent like a canvas fly
Stitched bright and tight
Across your valley...

    While a check wind whispers
        Through the poles of your tipi,
            Sheltering the long thighs of her dozing mountain.

On late summer evenings when it's still,
Down Chopaka past Loomis to Sarsapkin,
Dipping nighthawks slice
And their slanting chorus buzzes and zaps...

    Brrzz rruup... brrzz rrip.

And it echoes and multiplies
In the cool pools of her springs
Smiling like kisses in the forest.

Written at Sarsapkin Creek near Forde Lake in the Sinlahekin Valley between Concunully and the town of Loomis, at the southern end of the Similkameen Sub-basin.

Sometimes My Mind Goes Outside Itself

Why ask where I am when I can always be with you,
Soaring in at the speed of light
To tickle your nose, caress your ankle,
Balance on the nape of your neck,
Glide across your collarbone, trickle to your navel.

When you sense me, I'll fill your eyes with sparks from my pupils;
I'll get inside your eardrums with my whispers;
I will dart like a greenling through the eelgrass of your hair,
To rest in the kelp of that sacred pool.

Written in West Seattle, 18 January 2003

Memories That Stay On
An anniversary poem for Chong-hui

It was thirteen years ago
we joined hands together,
    feeding the seagulls on Elliott Bay.

Since then you and I have slept under
three hundred and seventy-three moons,
    breathing the same sweet air.

We've planted over a hundred trees
around the old bungalow on Holden Street,
    and made a tall forest grow out of our kneeholes.

We've found a numinous notch in the foothills
where the Little Mosquito pours out of its canyon
    all year long into the valley of the Okanogan.

We've made a home here for our spirits
entwined with coyotes in sagebrush under the aspen trees
    and we've learned how to talk to the clouds forming up over us,

Clouds that watch us,
and leave their gifts behind:
    the memories that stay on.

Written at Coyote Springs Farm, 17 August 2011.

Clovelly's Cyclone

He rides the ridge past North Elkhorn Creek,
and heads due north for old Monterey Station
by the canebrake, above Paris, chasing his moon shadow
on a fast chestnut stallion called Clovelly's Cyclone.

Maybe it's a dream on a cool summer night,
when the bourbon quiets the lightning out Russell Cave Road;
but mornings you can still hear his dream horse thundering
through the fog down in Houston Creek beyond Jacoby's Curve
under Boone's Blue ashes through the Buffalo clover
across the savanna behind old Bill Thompson's farm.

Written at Clovelly Farm on the North Elkhorn River along the Paris Pike Highway between Fayette County and Bourbon County, Kentucky, July 2000.

A Night with the Saguaros

Driving all day across the Sonoran Desert
on the way to Tucson, I pulled over to sleep
under a few old Saguaros that stood off the road
clustered in the boulders.

They were tall, their branching arms bejeweled
with white-yellow flowers, the petals tough enough
to hold the toes of white-winged doves,
or the claws of Long-nosed Bats, their nighttime
pollinating dance partners.

The saguaros seemed to look down at me, probing:
"We're nine-tenths water just like yourself
and we've been standing here a very long time."

Pumping out clouds of the monsoons of August:
"What can you bring?"
"The bats don't come anymore to sip our flowers.
"D'you know where they've gone?"

They think I don't know they wonder about these things:
"Who are you? We're watching you," they say.
"Why don't you stop to talk? Listen to dove's call.
Quail's like a clock.
Rattler sleeps like a stick on a rock."

Swiveling like sextants they seem to ask:
"Watch the stars inch past our arms,
We're older than your great grandparents
who you also ignored as much.
You're the last ones who can save us.
You still have time."

"Sit down and rest," they say.
"Make up a song.
Give us long life and save yourselves."
"The wind carries your stories and songs,
But it won't take long
Before your bones are chalk."

Written with the Carnegiea 48igantean in the Sonora Desert east of Sells, Arizona,
8 April 2011.

Kisses from the Highlands

This morning, after breakfast, proud-faced, stair-stepping,
Rock-cliffed Mt. Hull started blowing warm kisses
South onto Whisky Mountain's puckered cheeks,
Causing, over our fields, the frozen Okanogan River's
Lingering, sleepy breath to turn all rimey
Way up her cottonwood skirts, as a cloud
Of riverfret condenses in the valley
And clamps every branch and twiggy-finger strumming
Along our creek into the lacy shadows of Full Moon's
Last tryst, before making the fresh, new
Lunar year* of what is, is.

Written at Coyote Springs Farm, Little Mosquito Creek Mosquito Creek in the North Okanogan Valley, 30 January 2013, in anticipation of the birthing new moon of the coming Lunar Year on the tenth of February, a Year of the Snake.

The Footbridge

The footbridge connects the house to the barn.
Sitting on it now my feet,
Like ducks in my creek,
Connect me to the North Pacific's spinning gyre
Like a battery that turns the world.
It changes my tide four times a day;
Last night's moon lifted fresh coconuts
Out of Wailua River on Kauai Island
And scattered them up Lumahai Beach to shade the lovers.
I'm reborn every time I go to the barn.

Written at Coyote Springs Farm,
Little Mosquito Creek-Okanogan Sub Watershed,
Okanogan River Sub Basin, Columbia River Basin, Washington.
22 March 2014

RIVERS HAVE A HEART

With age, your muscles can weaken and become laced with fat. Or, they can get more sinewy from each landscape experience, braided with cords that got stronger but relaxed in their length from all the turns you made. Also, as years go by, you find you can pull off to rest and sleep anywhere, and wake restored and expand to breach old barriers or discover new channels. Your male and female halves can also entwine like clouds and rivers sometime laminate together, feed each other and restore each other. Every piece of every landscape is part of a watershed and very surface faces downstream out to the sea (some inward to dead seas). Gravity swings everything, including you and me, and makes your clock keep ticking. You and I are also tributaries of our community watersheds. I moved out of the city because it was becoming generic, it's new people more intolerant and regionally dumb, looking to imitate not be their unique selves. The city was starting to eat itself like a carnivorous flower. I felt like I was dying and I had to get out.

I chose to settle in a more diversified culture, in a physiographic region with colliding ecologies. It's where the largest county (Okanogan) in Washington joins one of the smallest (Ferry). It's known as the Okanogan Country, where the North Cascades Sub-Continent collides with the Okanogan/Kettle Highlands of the Columbia Mountains Sub-Continent, crushing it against the Northern Rocky Mountains, the original Pacific shore of North America. All of this happens within a hundred miles. Coniferous Rainforests, Alpine Meadows, Aspen Springs, Tamarack Parklands, Ponderosa Savannas, Sagebrush Steppes, Bunchgrass Prairies, Bitterbrush Deserts, Cottonwood Galleries and Riverine Grasslands, tightly woven across this rumpled network of ridges between sequestered hidden valleys.

Braided River

Maybe if I'd kept on going to that big doctor in Seattle,
I'd have died a long time ago.
But lifting the old handle of the pitcher-pump seven times
lifts a gallon of water, cold and clear
from twelve feet down the hand-dug homestead
well and carry it back to the house to eat
four apples from our tree each morning with the hand
ground coffee before I shave and brush my teeth,
before we feast on the radishes, onions, and tomatoes
and the peppers we brought in for Chong's strong hand's
to chop into her magical Sockeye kimchi
bursting now in my mouth like the Nesbitt's orange pop
I liked as a kid. That's what saved me!
And I'm so glad I'm still here, joyous to be alive.

Coyote Springs Farm
Mouth of the Canyon of the Little Mosquito
Okanogan Sub Basin

Sleeping on Rocks

    We lie,
here in the noonday sun
a couple of shadows on the forehead of Heggie's Rock,
    asleep,
It's dry where we are;
Wet skins of water beside us
    seep
off this granite dome, the rock itself
like last week's petrified storm still
    melts,
in drifts laid the day before yesterday
when it migrated past here,
    pelted.
We grow together beside other islands,
Other flowering communities that
    Swell.
Each drift expresses itself generation after generation;
As part of the same tapestry, it
    flowers
as we leave a few grains of love
on the granite bed we've chosen that now
    dissolve,
grains of love that make
their way into vernal pools to
    nourish
the five-petalled, white Minuartia,
and crimson corollas and
    ooze
rainbows to the clouds that bunch
up over us like Elders as they
    pass.

Written while at Heggie's Rock, off the Old Louisville Road in Appling, Columbia County in the Piedmont of Georgia, 7 March 2010.

The Landscape of Love's Fruiting Mind

Every time
You sing a love song,
Speak my name to the sun,
Every time
You kiss the wind,
Smile at birds watching you,
Or talk to flowers in the rain,
My pollen will fall
From the clouds by day and the stars by night,
To settle in the stigmas of your long black hair
And feed the landscapes of your sweet fruiting mind.

Written in West Seattle, 14 February 2004.

Open Thine Eyes: Talking to Beaverhead

You are not alone
This moment
It waits
Until your awake
It's always there
But where have you been?

And there you are
Part of everything
But changed
Transformed
Searching
Then where'd it go?

There is no other
It won't come back here again
It's everywhere
It's the space between
But never call it nothing
Because it's everything.

It's watching
It's listening
It's holding you up
It's lifting you
It pulls you on
It's gravity itself.

It's in your heart
It's inside you head
It's a spirit
It's you
It's me
There is no other.

It's not the future
It's not the past
It's before
It's beyond
It's now
Is that all there is to it?

It's in your eyes
In your hair
In your fingers
All across your skin
And it pulses in your hands
And in theirs—your friends and lovers.

It's in your breath
It makes words come out of nowhere
It remembers everything
It remembers me
It remembers you
It gives you a voice.

It forgets nothing
It's all around you
But you can't own it
But it waits
It feels your feelings
Are you connected?

Why do you wonder so?
Why do you struggle?
Why are you lost?
Why do you feel guilty?
Where do get the idea you've sinned?
Nothing is wrong. Open your eyes.

Respect your Mountain's presence
It remembers your love
Shine out yourself so that it can see you
Feels its breath when it cools you in the evening
It's heart pounds strongest if you open your eyes
Give it a nod before turning in: "Sleep Well, Mountain!"

"Good Morning," Mountain of my dreams.
"You're looking good. Better than you should."
Considering what you know by now
Of the general state of human affairs,
From Aeneas to Anchorage and from Antwyne to Albuquerque,
Let alone from Astoria to Angkor Wat,
Or Alderwood Manor to Amboseli or, you know what I mean—
And we're still in the first letter of the alphabet.

But the creek keeps chuckling with gifts from your springs,
Colder and clearer each year you've been watching us;
And the snowflakes this morning swirling off your brow
Gather and braid up like the Cottonwood seeds
Make drifts along our road to the barn each spring,
Or the way Chokecherries blow blossoms on our pond like brush strokes.
That's how you talk back to us, and why I reply in this poem.
"Thanks, Beaverhead!"

Written at Coyote Springs Farm at the mouth of the Canyon of the South Fork of Mosquito Creek, under Beaverhead Mountain, North Okanogan Valley, Washington
4 February 2014

Mapping Marriage Places
For Martha Wyckoff and Jerry Tone

I map their creeks, their wetted ravines,
their unwetted swales, ridges,
cheeks, dimples, swells, and rises,
their outcrops and balds,
glades and openings,
rest circles and the view
spots at their big trees and rocks;

Then I plot their marriage places for shelters,
tipis, cabins, deck platforms,
guest houses and even gravesites if they like.
This gets them thinking about these spots
as spiritual spots, marriage places with their land,
and it gets them thinking about the trails in between.

After a few of these conversations,
they begin to call them out,
give them names.
Words stick.
Their hands touch.
The land says:
Thanks.

Inspired by Martha and Jerry and their Swauk Prairie Farm, on Night Creek, Teanaway River, Upper Yakima River Sub Basin.

Strong As A Willow
For Chong-hui

Our old willow holds its green leaves longer this year.
It does this to honor your bathing beneath its ancient trunk
Because the spring water that washes your hair
Feeds its deepest roots with the same energies that make
You stronger each year that you take care of this place
At the mouth of the canyon, where we found our eternal love.

Coyote Springs
Mouth of the Canyon of the Little Mosquito
North Okanogan Valley
November 9, 2014

You Bent My River

My spirit body grew in a direction like a river.
First in the buried branch under a glacier,
the north face of the sleeping volcano.
Second in the branch below snowfields hanging
off the west face racing down the slick,
mossy chutes through boulders.
Third in the branch from bubbling springs
cleaving the sandstone cheeks
of this ancient island that migrated from Siberia.
My branches joined in ever-widening braidworks,
islands among islands,
logjams twined with channels seeking oneness to unfurl broadly,
to unwind their laminated and milty
serpentine muscle across a widening plain.
Finally my meanders shifted northward,
looping reaches built their own dikes with bow-wash momentum
seeking the estuarine sea, but bedrock sills kept lifting to drag me;
then rising storms and floods broke
breaching my banks like brimming waterfalls.
Finally I was lost down a long
crescent oxbow and I had to back out to find my way
Then you rose out of nowhere, stared at me
with your beaver-hair bristled and glistening,
so pleased you'd built a dam one night to catch me.
You wore a dark leather vest, its black tufts blooming
from armholes like marmots under your shoulders.
The three white streaks in your raven-feather hair
were lightning trails off the steppes of Mongolia.
But your smile really stopped me, bent my river
south into the sun. And we're here now
together, forever in the delta of this marriage.

Mouth of the Okanogan River
Big Bend of the Columbia

Falling in Love with Land Is Not Easy to Explain

I guess it was the creek that captured me first.
I fell in love with sky second.
Then rock outcrops and escarpments,
Then trails and scattered trees.

Down in the valley where we are, no forest exists—
Gallery ribbons with red-twigged dogwood,
River birch and a few cottonwoods.
Skeins of aspen tremble and quake,
Underground rootlets springing out of the ground
Around the seeps that perch
Along benches of hill slopes, but otherwise

It's all bunchgrass and sagebrushes
With bitterbrush that sometimes we call greasewood.
The greasewoods are blooming now with creamy flowers.
It's a harsh community with ticks and rattlers
So it's not so easy to fall in love with.

There's sadness too in our dying
Ponderosas who've survived so long
So long careening out from cracks in cliffs!
But now in rising heat and desiccation
They're succumbing to bark beetles—
And slowly turn brassy green before collapsing.

It's more like this landscape survives and doesn't complain,
Causing you to take stock of your own precious
Fragile and tough body, love it more and respect it
For its own persistence and scrappy survival.
Of course it's made us love our marriage partnership as well.
We became the pioneer pair who will be buried here,
Pair who've rooted in and made a home.

It's kind of scary sometimes.
But it's also the way it is, the way things have to be.
So we decided to love it for its self, ugly or not,
Beautiful or not, common, singularly unique body.

It's so complicated and simple simultaneously.
Small chunks of hornblende granite spall
Off our cheeks into the lips of the coulee after dark.
Am I making sense?

Coyote Springs Farm
Mouth of the Canyon of the Little Mosquito
30 April 2015

I've Been This Way All My life

I've been this way all my life;
I listened to rivers, learned to sing.
Sat with ancient cedars in the rain
Watched raindrops become rivulets in fissures of bark
Transposed, transfigured, transmigrated,
Transmutated,
Become a river.
It isn't so easy to be a river.
Even though trees talk to you, widen your span;
And you whisper back under their arches,
People can't hear you do this.
But birds seem to know.
Rocks breathe.
Peaks and mesas undress.
Talus blooms rare butterflies. Pikas whistle.
Mountains watch for signs of respect
To cry when ignored, even moan.
So I share what I know
With those who fly,
Swim, crawl and walk,
Sway, shimmer, sough and quake.
But those who talk out loud
Have lost their ears for this kind of music.
I'm a shaman,
Share what I see, what I hear.
I write poems as a way to converse without ridicule.
The land gives my inner voice,
Feels the weight of me out on the ledges.
The river covers my tracks in the sand.

Coyote Springs Farm
Mouth of the Canyon of the Little Mosquito

Rivers Have A Heart
Conversation between Mike Robinson and Grant Jones

Mike *'Limus:"*

*If a river has a heart,
is this what gathers salmon?...
When salmon lash themselves,
pass waterfalls.*

Grant *'Thalweg:"*

*The trees pump the water to the sky and haul
the sun-blood back into the Earth;
Together, the water and the sun-blood,
flutter inside each watershed.
The salmon are the hemoglobin
in the arteries of the river being.
You can breathe to their
pulse.*

Written at Coyote Springs Farm while corresponding with Mike Robinson at Milo's Meander and Thames' Creek above the Dash Point Reach Beach, South Central Sound Sub Region, Central Puget Sound Region.

Spirit Visitors

They passed behind a broken tree,
the walnut shaking in the wind.
One moved hunched on four legs
low in grass dried out brown
color of dirt. The other fluttered
followed smaller, like tumbleweed
bounced off its leader, trailing his shadows.
Shadows—or their shifts—in afterlight?
That's what I saw I guess, shadows.
But then the big one's eyes burned through my Filson
tin vest, cooked its paraffin
sweet enough to eat.

Coyote Springs Farm
Mouth of the Canyon of the Little Mosquito

At the River

At the river
I sit, heels in her bank
And watch who's watching,
Sleep on her boulders,
Stand in her.
Walking upstream across her,
Trembling with her,
I have learned to traverse her
And come back from the other side.
Resonating inside her,
I communicate through her,
Sharing her presence,
Her mist rising,
Her clouds forming
Under his kissing rain.
Tasting my own tears,
I bushwack through her branches
Always staying within earshot.
I've learned her lessons,
Following my heart,
Never letting go,
Never rusting out.

Coyote Springs
Mouth of the Canyon of the Little Mosquito
North Okanogan Valley

View from the Eyebrow Bench of Coyote Springs Farm across the Riverbraids Arboretum Gardens to the looped meanders of the Okanogan River

Your Stories

Each landscape offers its own story. Each landscape is a book that's open to any observer who's awake. Each landscape carries the language to describe itself; in fact the biologic foundations present in the landscape are the vocabulary of the local language in our own place. Everything you can say about your place derives there and has its origin in what you can see.

The rocks and the trees, and the rivers and animals in the landscape are the words and phrases, sentences and paragraphs. Together these rocks and words comprise the full discourse of your exchange with it. If you don't know its features you can't converse with it. In other words you're a partner at the table with your local landscape and if you're open you can hear each other. The more you see and describe the better you can listen. The landscape's spirits will weave with the life energies inside each one of us if we are awake with her in the present moment.

It's for these reasons that I see and hear everything around me as a poetic structure. I see the landscape of a place as the architecture of a poem.

Each landscape makes the language, and the language it makes can save it. Each landscape depends on you for its survival, and your life depends on this relationship. You're its steward and interpreter.

To communicate our feelings toward those whom we love, the landscape we share gives us the full range of metaphor and depth of meaning we wish to celebrate in our human relationships.   GJ

My Place

This is the heart of back-to-the-land, organic orchards, and open-range ranchlands. Several small town necklaces follow the streamways around here: Brewster, Bridgeport, Nespelem, Inchelium and Kettle Falls follow the Columbia; Keller, Aeneas and Republic up the Sanpoil; Monse, Mallot, Okanogan, Omak, Riverside, Tonasket, Oroville and Loomis up the Okanogan-Similkameen; Pateros, Carlton, Twisp, Winthrop and Mazama up the Methow; and Chesaw, Malo and Danville up the Myers and Curlew of the Kettle. These comprise the supply valleys for organic food (fruit, vegetables, and meat) to the Puget Lowlands (The Salish Sea Megalopolis). It's also one of the most culturally diversified belief-landscapes in the West. Whereas the Salish Sea urban metropolis is almost uniformly democratic, North Central Washington is American Indian, Mexican-American, Buddhist, Christian, Agnostic, Hippie, Escapist, Liberal, Conservative, Cowboy, Logger, Rancher, Orchardist, Organic Farmer, Artist-Singer, Writer, Teacher, Doctor, Rich, Pension-Retired and Dirt Poor, all living in harmony with each other in positive tolerance of each others values. Eastern Washington (Spokane) is more rightwing. Coastal Washington (Seattle-Tacoma) people don't differentiate or tolerate.

Wherever you are, I hope you become your own river, because there's nothing like you.   **Grant Jones**

"Advance confidently in the direction of your dreams...
endeavor to live the life you have imagined...
as you simplify your life,
the laws of the universe will appear less complex..."

H.D. Thoreau, *Walden*
US Transcendentalist 1817-1862

Grant Jones at Coyote Springs Far   C. Jones

The Author

Grant Jones, born August 29, 1938, grew up on a beachfront farm at Richmond Beach in the northern reaches of the Central Puget Sound Region of the Salish Sea Estuary. His father, Victor, was Welsh-Irish Canadian and his mother, Ione, was Quaker English-Irish American. He began writing poetry at the age of eleven, but found his unique voice as one of Theodore Roethke's poets in the fabled Advanced Verse Writing Class Roethke conducted from 1961 to 1964 as Poet in Residence at the University of Washington. Jones is Founding Principal of Jones & Jones Architects, Landscape Architects and Planners, Ltd., with Ilze Grinbergs Jones in 1969 and Johnpaul Jones in 1972, maintaining an international design practice in the historic Globe Building in Pioneer Square Seattle over the last forty-five years. Since 2006 he has made his home in the North Okanogan Valley of North Central Washington, where he and his wife Chong-hui created the Jones Riverbraids Arboretum Gardens at Coyote Springs Farm in Ellisforde between Tonasket and Oroville.

His landscape poetry is recognized as a fundamental part of his intrinsic design approach and integral to his research and scholarship in landscape architecture and ecological design. He is an Affiliate Professor in the Department of Landscape Architecture at the College of Built Environments (CBE), University of Washington. Jones has held teaching positions at Harvard, the University of Oregon, UC Berkeley, University of Virginia and Texas A&M, and lectured at thirty-five universities on ecological design, landscape planning and poetry. He is the recipient of the *President's Award of Excellence* from ASLA and 100 awards from ASLA, AIA, APA, ASHTO, AZA, AABGA, including forty awards for zoo and wildlife park design. His firm is *First Recipient* of *The Firm of the Year Award* from ASLA. He and Ilze Jones won the *Richard Neutra Medal* from CalPoly Pomona. He was *First Recipient of The LAF Medal* from the Landscape Architecture Foundation. He is a Frederick Sheldon Fellow of Harvard University, and Glimcher Fellow of the Knowland School of Architecture, The Ohio State University. He was inducted to the Roll of Honor, College of Built Environments at the University of Washington in April of 2015.

Several poems in this collection have been published in: *What Rocks Know selected poems of Grant Jones, Okanogan Poems Volume 1, Okanogan Poems Volume 2 seventeen poets, Okanogan Poems Volume 3 landscapes are observatories,* Skookumchuck Press; *The Fullness,* Landscape Journal; *Seeing, Where Logic and Feelings Meet,* Landscape Architecture Magazine; *Grant Jones: A Plan for Puget Sound,* Princeton Architectural Press Sourcebook 4 by Jane Amidon; and *The Methow Naturalist, two poems, 18.1, 20.4.* George Thompson Publishing (GFT) will publish his book, *Listening to the Voice of the Earth,* a collection of stories, sketches and poems, including several in this limited collection, in 2018.

Photo of Coyote Springs Farm Sign arc-cut and welded by Jane Thompson

www.ingramcontent.com/pod-product-compliance
Lightning Source LLC
Chambersburg PA
CBHW080546090426
42734CB00016B/3221